Welcome 'To
JAPAN

COPYRIGHT

Welcome
TO JAPAN

> ## Hello there, daring youngster!
> Are you ready to go on an exciting experience right in your backyard? Prepare to discover the wonders of Japan, a country rich in old temples, bustling cities, and unique cultures. Japan has so much to offer, from ninja methods to scrumptious food, and vivid festivals to entertaining anime characters. Take a map, gather your adventure gear, and let's explore the wonderful world that awaits you now that you have your very own Japan travel guide for kids! The journey has started!

ALL ABOUT ME

This is a picture of me ⤵

My name is
_____
- - - - - - - - - - - - - - - -
_____

I am _____ years old.

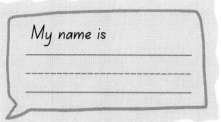

Which country are you from?
_____

Who are you travelling with
_____

Which place in Japan are you most excited about? Why?

1 _____

2 _____

3 _____

CONTENT

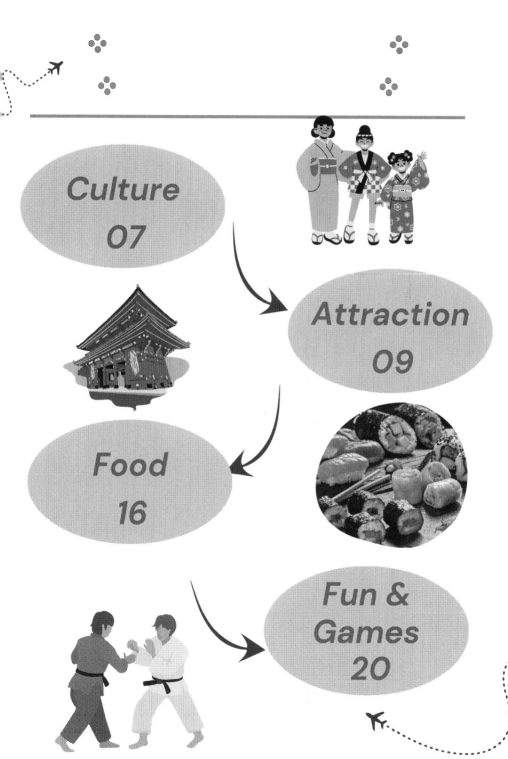

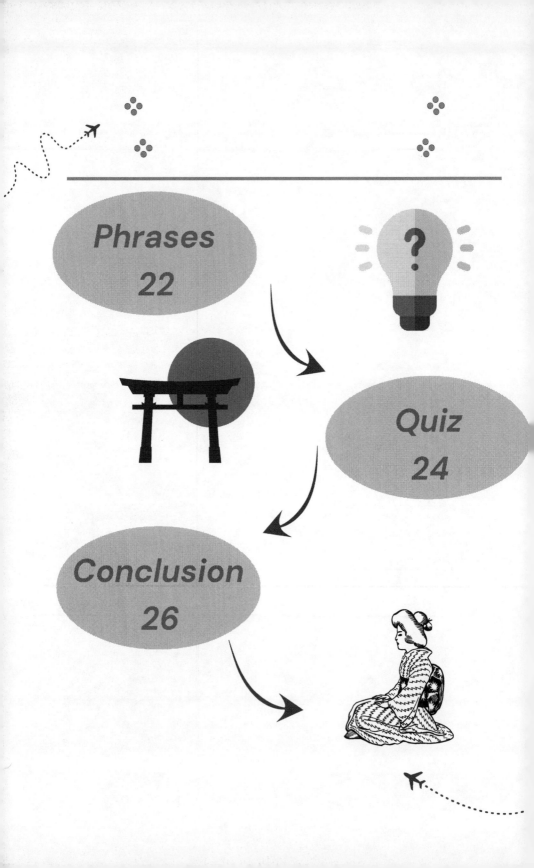

GEOGRAPHY

Japan is an archipelago, or collection of islands, situated near Asia's most eastern tip. Kyushu, Shikoku, Honshu, and Hokkaido are the four main islands. There are also over 4,000 little islands! Russia's Siberian region is Japan's nearest neighbor on the continent, with Korea and China farther south.

Mountains cover over four-fifths of Japan. Honshu is the largest island, with the Japanese Alps running through its center. Mount Fuji, a cone-shaped volcano revered by many Japanese, is the highest mountain.

Japan might be a dangerous place. Three of the tectonic plates that make up the Earth's crust overlap nearby and often grind against one another, causing earthquakes. Every year, more than a thousand earthquakes strike Japan. In Japan, there are over 200 volcanoes, 60 of which are active.

Japan is an island country on the Asian continent. Japan is an archipelago or group of islands that run along Asia's eastern border from the northern coast of Russia to the South China Sea.

The Japanese islands are made up of four main islands and numerous smaller ones. There are around 6,800 islands in all. Honshu, the world's seventh-largest island, is the largest of the four major islands. Tokyo, Yokohama, Osaka, and Nagoya are Japan's four major cities.
Mount Fuji, Japan's highest mountain, is a dormant (sleeping) volcano whose last eruption occurred in 1707. Mount Fuji is 3,776 meters/12,388 ft tall.

Tokyo is 8 hours by aircraft from Singapore, 13 hours from London, and 12.5 hours from New York.

FAST FACTS

- OFFICIAL NAME: Japan
- FORM OF GOVERNMENT: Parliamentary government with a constitutional monarchy
- CAPITAL: Tokyo
- POPULATION: 126,168,156
- OFFICIAL LANGUAGE: Japanese
- MONEY: Japanese yen
- AREA: 145,883 square miles (377,835 square kilometers)
- MAJOR MOUNTAIN RANGES: Japanese Alps
- MAJOR RIVERS: Biwa, Inawashiro, Kasumigaura

HISTORY

Japan was first populated some 30,000 years ago. People used to go between the big islands since Siberia and Korea were connected by dry-land bridges at the time. The first culture, the Jomon civilization, developed some 12,000 years ago. The Ainu people came at the same time, traveling by sea from Siberia.

The Jomon and Ainu have survived for thousands of years through hunting, fishing, and gathering plants. Around 300 B.C., the Yayoi people landed on Honshu Island from China and Korea. They were skilled toolmakers, weavers, and farmers who began producing rice in flooded paddy fields.

In 660 B.C., Japan's first emperor, Jimmu Tenno, ascended to the throne. Japan was ruled by emperors until the 12th century A.D. Then military officers known as shoguns seized power and governed by force.

The first Europeans arrived in Japan in 1543, bringing guns and Christianity. In 1635, the governing shogun prohibited Japanese people from leaving the nation. This solitude lasted more than 200 years. In 1868, the shoguns were deposed, and the emperors were restored. This was an era of great modernization and transition in Japan.

During World War I (1914-1917), Japan fought with the Americans. However, on December 7, 1941, Japan attacked Pearl Harbor in Hawaii, prompting the US to declare war on Japan and begin World War II. From 1941 until 1945 Japanese military leaders participated in warfare with American and coalition soldiers. In August 1945, the United States dropped atomic bombs on the Japanese cities of Hiroshima and Nagasaki, killing about 115,000 people. Japan officially submitted it a few days later.

03

WEATHER

If you're considering taking a trip to Japan and would want to know the weather prediction, you may get it here:

1. SPRING (MARCH THROUGH MAY)

Temperature:

Mild to chilly, ranging from 10 to 20 degrees Celsius (50 to 68 degrees Fahrenheit).

Clothing:

Layers and a lightweight jacket or sweater are recommended. Bring an umbrella in case it rains.

2. SUMMER (JUNE TO AUGUST)

- **Temperature:**

Warm to hot, around 25-35°C (77-95°F)

- **Clothing:**

Wear light, breathable clothes such as t-shirts, shorts, and dresses. Don't forget sunscreen and a hat for protection from the sun.

❖

3. AUTUMN (SEPT TO NOV)

- **Temperature:**

Mild to cool, around 10-20°C (50-68°F)

❖

- **Clothing:**

Similar to spring, layering is recommended. Bring a light jacket or sweater for cooler days.

❖

4. WINTER (DECEMBER TO FEBRUARY)

- **Temperature:**
Cold, around 0–10°C (32–50°F)
- **Clothing:**
Bundle up with a warm coat, hat, gloves, and scarf. It can also snow in some parts of Japan, so bring appropriate footwear.

5. TYPHOON SEASON (AUGUST TO OCTOBER)

·Japan experiences typhoons (tropical cyclones) during this period. They can bring heavy rain and strong winds. Pay attention to weather reports and follow any instructions from local authorities.

Check the weather forecast and plan accordingly before embarking on your excursion. It's a good idea to be prepared for unexpected weather changes at all times. Have a great time in Japan!

PEOPLE & CULTURE

The Japanese are well-known for their propensity to work hard. Children are taught to respect others, especially their parents and superiors. They learn to prioritize the needs of their family or company before their own.

Western and Japanese cuisines are quite different from one another. There is little meat, but plenty of rice, fish, and vegetables. This diet, which contains very little fat or dairy, is very healthy and leads to Japanese people enjoying the world's longest lives on average.

NATURE

The Japanese people treasure the beauty of the countryside. According to the ancient Shinto religion, natural phenomena such as mountains, waterfalls, and forests contain spirits or souls.

Rural regions cover the majority of Japan. However, wildlife has suffered as a result of more than 100 million people squeezed into such a small region.

Even though pollution is now rigorously controlled, road development and other human initiatives have ruined natural places. There are 136 endangered species in Japan.

A colder stream from the north joins the heated Tsushima stream on its way to the Sea of Japan. Fish and other marine life are numerous in the waters surrounding Japan due to water mixing.

Japan
DESTINATIONS

TOP ATTRACTION

Because it offers urban wonders, nature, cultural activities, entertainment, and leisure facilities, Japan is an attractive location for families traveling with children. The following activities may be added to a day trip or vacation by local families.

Shrines & Temples

Japan has around 90,000 temples and a corresponding number of shrines. Many of them are local hangouts that serve as oases. Others are among Japan's most magnificent sights.

Theme Parks

Hundreds of theme parks, both huge and small, dot the landscape of Japan. Among the major parks are well-known attractions like Disneyland and Universal Studios, as well as distinctive Japanese attractions such as Fuji-Q Highland.

Onsen

Visiting onsen hot springs is the most popular hobby in Japan. Weekend trips to the country are common among city dwellers who like nature.

The Japanese see onsen as a cultural and community activity that is essential for the socialization of youngsters. Onsen bathtubs are often gender-specific, and you must enter the bath nude. Young children should enter the bath with an adult on the other side. Certain large onsen resorts include onsen pools where you may dress for the water.

Towns & Villages

Aside from nature, beaches, parks, onsen, castles, temples, and historical sites, Japan has a plethora of attractive little towns with quiet streets.

Observation Decks

Almost every Japanese city has at least one observation deck with a panoramic view of the city. By far the greatest is Tokyo's Skytree.

Japanese Castles

Japan has around 100 castles, the bulk of which are modern reconstructions of ancient buildings, with a few originals remaining standing.
Some castles have a castle tower and extensive moat defense systems.

The Shinkansen

Traveling by bullet train may be exciting and handy for children. Although there isn't much space for luggage on the Shinkansen, you can still travel to your hotel.

Skiing & Snowboarding

Japan has hundreds of ski resorts, many of which are ideal for beginners and little children. Skiers with more expertise may also discover greater res. Deep p: the best circumstances are frequently found during peak season. There is a lot of skiing in the prefectures of Nagano and Niigata, which are both close to Tokyo. Most hotels provide rentals as well as lessons.

Sport

Baseball and soccer are the two most popular spectator sports in Japan. Nippon Professional Baseball games are enjoyable in cities with large fan bases, such as Nagoya. J. League, the country's professional soccer league, is made up of 18 teams. Although these games sometimes sell out months in advance, it is possible to see the national squad play international matches. is another option, however, youngsters typically find it slow. The days pass slowly, from early morning to late afternoon. Sumo demonstrations and open practices, which are typically free, may be equally appealing to children.

Hanami

Hanami, which translates to "flower viewing," is the Japanese ritual of having a party under cherry trees when they bloom in the spring. The term may also allude to a walk in the woods. Cherry blossom season is Japan's favorite seasonal event, and e longs to be outdoors among the trees. Some Hanami venues may be loud and congested with drunk partygoers. Smaller neighborhood sports and parks with limited hours, such as Shinjuku Gyoen in Tokyo, are often quieter..

Beaches

Many of Japan's best beaches are close to Tokyo, including those in Chiba, Kanagawa, and Izu. The majority of nations, including Japan, enjoy a short beach season from late August to late July. Each has its character, with some functioning as summer party centers and others attracting solely families. In general, party beaches like Shonan are less popular with families and more popular with surfers.

Festivals of Yosakoi

Yosakoi is a festival dance that combines both modern and traditional elements. This recess, its popularity has risen, and practically every institution and college in Japan has a team. Hundreds of teams compete in a single event, with the majority having over 100 dancers apiece. Yosakoi dancing gatherings are often cheerful and joyful.

Creating Mochi

Moc, a sticky kind of Japanese rice, was traditionally hammered with wooden mallets to make chewy rice cakes known as mochi. This traditional method is still utilized on special occasions such as New Year's. It is available to children as a CC cultural activity at festivals, resort hotels, and tourist places in Japan.

Yukata

During Hanabi and summer festivals, traditional cotton robes known as yukata are worn. Children's yukata are inexpensive and easy to obtain at department shops or outlet malls throughout the season. Kids like the sense of cultural immersion that wearing yukata provides.

Islands

The Okinawan Islands stand out among Japan's numerous gorgeous islands due to their intriguing indigenous culture and magnificent beaches.

Strolling

Given that mountains cover the bulk of the country, hiking is a popular sport in Japan. There are paths, both short and lengthy, in every corner of the country.

Purchasing

Japan features a variety of family-friendly shopping areas with a unique range of toys and clothing for children. Many department stores provide a children's floor and practical features such as rooftop playgrounds and roomy family restrooms. Many shopping areas have packed and tiny pathways.

Snow Festivals

Every winter, the Japanese regions of Tohoku and Hokkaido organize a variety of snow festivals that feature kid-friendly activities, performances, and snow sculptures. The Sapporo Snow Festival is without a doubt the largest.

Japanese FOOD

MOST POPULAR FOOD ❖

Rice, fish, soy products, and vegetables are staples of the Japanese diet. These ingredients are found in a variety of dishes, including soups and sushi.
Popular Japanese dishes include:

Teriyaki

Teriyaki is a dark, sticky sauce flavored with honey, ginger, garlic, an soy sauce.

Taiyaki

Taiyaki is a delectable cake dish shaped like a fish.

MOST POPULAR FOOD

Sushi & Sashimi

These delicate rice rolls or small morsels of raw fish, shellfish, or vegetables.

Tempura

Tempura is a light and crispy deep-fried food that includes fried vegetables, fish, shellfish, and meat.

Yakitori

Skewered chicken pieces that are often dunked in salty soy sauce.

MOST POPULAR FOOD

Bento Box:

Lunchboxes that often feature sushi and other delectable treats and snacks.

Ramen

Ramen is a form of thin egg noodles that are often served in broth.

Soba

Soba are buckwheat noodles that are often served in broth. Beef and seafood dishes are popular culinary partners for this sauce.

FUN & GAMES ●

❖ *Ichimatsu Dolls*

Ichimatsu dolls are popular Japanese children's toys. Ichimatsu dolls, which come in a range of sizes and shapes, have been around since the Edo period. Children may pretend to run a company, dress up, and participate in several other fun activities.

Origami ❖

Paper folding, often known as origami, is a popular activity among young Japanese people. Children may draw whatever form they choose, including animals and flowers. It's a fun and educational hobby that promotes creativity and patience.

❖ *Karuta*

A card game that has been played in Japan since the 16th century. In this amusing game, children must use their memory and observation abilities to find the proper card.

Kite

Kite flying is a traditional Japanese activity. Children like building kites and testing their altitude limitations. The Japanese are very welcoming and will help anybody who is just starting with kite flying!

Daruma Dolls

These traditional Japanese dolls are thought to bring good fortune. Children like sketching their pictures and decorating them with bright colors. They are also useful when kids are working hard and need some luck!

Top Spinning

Another traditional Japanese activity is top spinning. Children may put their endurance to the test by spinning a top on a string. Reflexes and coordination are pushed to the ultimate test.

Jump Rope

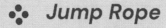

Jumping rope is popular in Japan. Children may compete against one another to determine who can jump the highest. Other alternatives include honing creative talents or seeing how far they can jump!

PHRASES

Konnichiwa

Hello!

Yes

Hai

Sayonara

Goodbye

PHRASES

Thank you
=
Arigatou

Please
=
Onegaishimasu

Where is…?
=
..wa doko desu ka?

Excuse me
=
Sumimasen

Quiz

What is the capital city of Japan?

How do you say "hello" in Japanese?

Name one famous Japanese food.

How many main islands make up Japan?

Name the tallest mountain in Japan.

What is the largest city in Japan?

How do you say "thank you" in Japanese?

CONCLUSION

Finally, the Children's Travel Guide for 2023 provides a comprehensive and fascinating resource for young visitors. This book aims to pique the attention of young readers and foster their love of travel by giving detailed information on a range of sites, interactive maps, and amusing activities. This book provides children with the knowledge and tools they need to go on exciting excursions throughout the world, whether they wish to explore historical landmarks, and natural wonders, or learn about different cultures. Let the Children's Travel Guide be their dependable travel companion as they experience the wonders of our diverse world in 2023 and beyond.

Thank You
ARIGATŌ

Made in the USA
Las Vegas, NV
28 February 2024

86415084R00023